The Gift of Love

The Gift of Love

La Shea A Stanard

iUniverse, Inc.
New York   Bloomington

The Gift of Love

iUniverse books may be ordered through booksellers or by contacting:

iUniverse
1663 Liberty Drive
Bloomington, IN 47403
www.iuniverse.com
1-800-Authors (1-800-288-4677)

ISBN: 978-1-4401-6309-8 (pbk)
ISBN: 978-1-4401-6308-1 (ebk)

Printed in the United States of America

iUniverse rev. date: 8/19/2009

DEDICATION

This book is dedicated to David with much love and respect.

INTRODUCTION

This book of poetry is about a single Christian woman and her faith. The poems reflect her love for Christ and her struggle as a single woman. She reflects on the world today, as she sees it. The poems also reflect her joy and pain of being in love with a man, and ultimately her acceptance of God's will for her life. I write this book to share and relate to other single Christian women and their struggle. I hope this book is a blessing to them or anyone who just enjoys a good book of poetry.

CONTENTS

COMING TRUE

All the unspoken wishes are at hand

The Desires of My Heart

A dying wish, a living wish

To be with the Father-Home

Yes, there was a plan

To save me and Humanity

To Live and Love-One Man

With all Humility

The Gift of Love

And to bare Joy to the world

This is how I praise My Lord

For I cannot praise Myself

My goal-to bring Dignity and Respect

To all Mankind

The Father holds All in His Right

Hand

Nothing shall be lost

And All shall be gained

Yes, Thou Heart's Desire shall be

Thine

Thank You Father from This Heart

Of mine

STRAIGHT FROM THIS HEART OF MINE

Thank You Father for this Heart of mine

And to raise my voice to You so high

To sing a song of Love and Praise

You taught me to Love in a Special Way

As an example for the world to see

To touch the hearts of those in need

Thank You Father forever more

My Father, I Praise You on high

Papa, Your ways are so Devine

Through my pain, through my tears, even my doubt

A seed sown, knew You would work it out

For my good and for Your Glory

You raised Me up

Against him, who wanted to push Me down

Oh Holy One on High!

I cry tears of Joy, which you gave to me

My cup runneth over, I cannot deny

I recompense a Love song to You

From the Heart and Soul of Your child

To them, You say, "She is of My Own"

No greater Love have I known

You brought the pain, You brought the tears

Only to make Me strong

The only way I know to thank You

Is through this song of mine

And to live my Life

By Righteousness and Truth

My cup runneth over and over because of You

Thank You Father for this Heart of mine

And to raise my voice to You so high

To sing a song of Love and Praise

You taught me to Love in a Special Way

As an example for the world to see

To touch the hearts of those in need

Thank You Father forever more

Thank You forever more

Thank You forever more

THIS FAITH

Oh what a mustard seed can do

It can move mountains

It can push fear aside

And encourage you

Oh what a mustard seed can do

You gave me courage to stand

In the midst of my fear

While my world was rolling away

But this Faith, wouldn't let me sway

All beholding to You

Oh what a mustard seed can do

It can move mountains

It can push fear aside

And encourage you

Oh what a mustard seed can do

You gave me a Love

That can withstand all

Yet so patient, but enduring all

I don't know the end of it all

But this Faith, I know will rejoice

In the end, it was worth it all

Oh what a mustard seed can do

It can move mountains

It can push fear aside

And encourage you

Oh what a mustard seed can do

NEAR TO THEE

You were there all the time

When I called out Your Name

You sent a star to guide my way

When I was rebellious,

Angels pushed demons out of my way

When I was sick in my body

You healed every part

When I was confused

You made my thoughts clear

Father, You were always near

Just to see You one day

Would be a blessing to my soul

When we finally embrace

And we stand face to face

"You are my Father"

"And you are my child"

I have finally made my way Home

HOME

Home is where your heart is

Home is where love abounds

Where stormy clouds never abound

Where family share hugs and kisses

And not a single little one misses

Sitting together enjoying favorite dishes

Voices raised together, rejoicing

God's bounty is beautiful

To be home at last

And no one can put you last

THE BAPTISMAL

What a happy day that was

Sitting on a pew, while smiling

Knowing, it was a decision

To always follow You

To show the world too

I gladly proclaim the truth

Of the One I believe in true

PERFECT LOVE

This Love I have in my heart

I will never let it part

From the Love You bestow upon me

So great, so unconditional

This Love shared from heart to heart

From the Father to His children

Perfect in all its ways

BRING BACK THE JOY

Bring back the Joy of yesterday

With a smile always on my face

And confidence in my pace

When my Love and I were one

And I believed our future

Had been won

Past Joy of being in my Father's House

Giving Him praise with all my Heart

Him lifting my soul to Himself at last

Oh, how I wish for the Joy of yesterday

Where three would be happy at last

But, I must trust His will for my life today

FEELING LONELY

Oh my Father, I know it's not Your wish

For me to be on this earth alone

I wonder- will I find myself Home?

All I want is to be in Your will

But Father, I'm starting to feel my age

And this waiting stage is a struggle uphill

Deep down inside, I do fear

There is no light at the end of the tunnel

With all honesty, I don't know what I need most now

But I know, You want this for me—

I wish to be the best I can be

THOU WILL BE DONE

Dear Father lead me, guide me

Everyone is waiting for me

I don't know what is expected

I don't know what to do

All I know is that I want to go Home

It seems that I can't get there alone

But I don't know what Your will is for me

Your power seems dormant in me

I beg You to help me do Your will

I know You are God

But I don't know if I should be still

Thou will be done

THE DEEP

I ask God, "where am I?"

I'm afraid to admit that I know

To the naked eye, all is fine

To the Spiritual One, all is maddening

They continue to ask Me- "why?"

"Do you not know?"

"Do you forget?"

I say, "I remember"

"Soon, I Will forget!"

HOPE

Who will be the last

Last to go Home

Do you believe?

Do you fear?

Have Faith in Me

So that We shall be happy in Peace

Dear Papa, I pray that things shall pass

Pass quickly

I know I shall not lose one

I place Mine first

So I humbly come to Thee Papa

Please bless me soon

For all eternity

GOODBYE

Goodbye to you, goodbye to the world

A world of lies

A world of hatred

A world of murder

A murder of the body

Worst of all, a murder of the Spirit

A world of fear

A world of crushing Faith?

Were they sure?

In my opinion, good riddens

And Good is hidden

Charity-where is She to be found?

THE WORLD

The land was blessed

The land was cursed

All at once

We had Faith

We had Hope

We had Charity—the Greatest of them All

After the curse, there was Grace

As it is written, "Saving Grace"

Grace has left

Now, one must get what he deserves

Hope is gone

Hope of not receiving what one deserves

Yes, there will be punishment

Free will is gone

Some cling to Faith—who's faith

There are true Angels in disguise, to protect Truth

Love for the world is gone

THEIR WORLD

A world gone all wrong

No longer a time to Love your neighbor

No longer a Guiding Light to a safe harbor

The road Home seems hard and long

One takes the high road

The other takes the low road

A decision made by the heart

Cold, hot, warm

Many forget Who can change

The mold

OLD-FASHIONED

A desire for yesterday instead

Of today

When the world was a caring one

Instead of a self-hating one

Children were happy and innocent

Not upset when receiving just a cent or two

When families ate together and prayed together

And stayed together

Instead of one out of two

Deciding not to keep it together

I wish for the time when, "gay," meant happy

And Love was an honest word

What will befall this world

In the day to come

THE DREAM

I never felt such joy

'til you preached the healing truth

Every Sunday went to Church

Just to hear the Word; it made me strong

Respect grew to Love

One day you told me His son Loves me

I dreamed of He and I in matrimony

Not side by side, but face to face

He smiling, but eyes closed

Now I wait to gaze into your eyes

Every morning and every kiss goodnight

REVELATION

This night so strong, so different

So close, but yet so far

For my Love to comfort me here tonight

I cry for the pain in my plight

And for the cold shoulder, I turn

To him or for Him I fight

A fight of not flesh and blood

But of Faith and Heart

For two to become three

And two to become one

And We All shall go Home

With a song in Our Heart

LOVE AND I

Love—so strong, so Wise

When my mind understands

But not my Heart

We shall put the pain behind

Down below, in the Deep

Then we can celebrate the Main Event

Two centered Hearts that beat as One

And moves as One...

When we make Love

And bring Joy to the world

TODAY, YESTERDAY

A youth of tears and heartache

Dug deep to heal the pain of yesterday

Along the way, a greater Love I did find

Unconditional for myself, and...

For Him and our Family in kind

WHEN

Oh my love, I miss you so

For me, there really is no substitute

'Tis your face I wish to see every day

To show you I love you in every way

I cried tears last night

Because of the distance apart

Each night my heart asks

When will we hold each other,

In the dark?

No longer a separation

But a consummation

Of our love

Of course I'll hold on 'til then

But I'll continue to ask you

When?

A LESSON ON TRUST

Dear little one, listen close

To a lesson

I'm still trying to grasp close

Some may say I'm a fool to say as such

But little one

I must be honest with you

And with myself as much

I believe within my heart

A strong foundation is the key

To know the Love of our Lord, and the Father God

To grow up Loved and secure indeed

If you stumble, if you fall

Just remember, you're never alone

Family is with you, where ever you go

Now little one

The trust between man and woman

Is a challenge I must admit

Be honest with yourself

And with him—always, if you do commit

There may be pain, you may even cry

But, He will respect you, and you will respect yourself in kind

Remember little one

Always be true to thineself first

Trust the Lord with all your heart, mind, and soul

And remember, with Him you have won

The peace and tranquility of life, sustained by love

Use these tools between you and your love

To live a life full of joy as one

A LOVE STORY

The night he found me, we embraced

With tears in my eyes and joy in my soul

He healed my soul with the wondrous Truth

Yet, did I know that he would be the one

To carry me Home, high in the sky

Then I was at here

And I missed him so

Searching for him

Each time the sun was high in the sky

But, he was nowhere to be found

Then one evening, he walked by with a, "hello"

Although awe on my face, there was joy in my soul

Then each day, I wondered when

Would I see him again

My heart hoped

But my soul already knew

He came to save me to anew

Then one wintery night

He found me again

All at once, tears rolled down my face

Respect turned to Love

Finally, I understood the passion

I felt for him inside

The same he felt for me, no longer did he hide

I cannot lie

There was some pain and tears along the way

With each test our love did abound

To bring us closer and not far away

Always abounding, never lacking for neither one

MY HEART

My dear mother, I've missed you so much

Since I've been here alone

Wishing for the time we could spend together

Even just to chat

To talk about issues

Only another woman could understand

Oh my dear mother, I cried last night

To speak to you

Believing you were so far away

Yearning to understand the pains of yesterday and last night

Then peace came to me at last

When I realized, you were always there

In my heart

And my love was just a phone call away

MOTHER

Mother Renee, I never felt your kiss, never felt your hug

Didn't you love me; didn't you want me

My heart is breaking because of a man

He left my side

Mother, how I need you now

Surely you understand such things some how

He's all I want

Do I compromise or do I hold my ground

Doesn't he love me; doesn't he want me

Mother, surely you understand such things some how

MISSING YOU

Oh my love, I miss you so

The feel of you near as close as one

To hear your voice and see your smile

Oh the memories are so sublime

Where are you; where did you go?

I dare not ask for your return

Because I don't know what's best for me

For my God understands and sees

I may not understand the reasons, now

I trust that it will all work out in the end

I do contemplate how

My spirit and heart will mend

All things work together for the good

And that's the way they always should

IS LOVE TOO GREAT

Here I am; I sit and wait

Waiting for you to come along

You said I was your only love

Was it all a dream?

Is love too great?

Do you ache; do you cry,

With a need so great?

Is love too great?

Here I am; I sit and wait

Waiting for you to come along

Am I not also worth the wait?

I thought I was your only best

Was it all a dream?

Is love too great?

NOW I SEE

Here I am; I sit and wait

Waiting for you to come along

You said you would never leave me

That you would always be with me

Was it all a dream?

Here I am; I sit and wait

Waiting for you to come along

Tears run down my face

Each day and each night

But you don't come to my dreams

Here I am; I sit and wait

Waiting for you to come along

Please, where did you go?

Now, I'm no longer

blind

You were with me all the time

Waiting for me to see

UNCONDITIONAL

My soul was in torment

My restless spirit wouldn't let me wait

My heartache was relentless

At my love's absence

I couldn't bear the weight

I need to be in his arms

I need his time; I need his passion

This is what I want from my love

My heartache turned to compassion

My prayers were answered, but not the way I expected

INTO MY LOVE'S EYES

When you look into your love's eyes

What do you see?

Do you see the brown on the bark of a tree

The brown of rich soil

Or the bright caramel as the sun

Comes up over the horizon

When you look into your love's eyes

What do you see?

Do you see the deep blue of the ocean

The light blue of the Heavens

Or do you see the universe

At his beck and command

When you look into your love's eyes

What do you see?

Do you see love, security, forever

I know I'll see the world as it will be

When I look into my love's Eyes

ABOUT THE AUTHOR

La Shea grew up mostly in southern New Jersey. Her love for writing began in high school, Cherry Hill High School West, where she attended for four years. Her writing was encouraged by winning several writing contests while attending high school. Her love for poetry grew by reading the classics of William Shakespeare. After a year of working, La Shea attended Rider University, where she received her Bachelor's of Science in Business Administration. She began writing poetry in her adult life through a crisis. It became a necessary outlet of her overwhelming emotions.

La Shea attended Church as a child. But in her teenage and early adult years, she became out of fellowship. She later rededicated her life to Christ in her early thirties. The bible says to raise up a child in the way that he should go, and when he gets older he will not depart.

The Gift of Love is La Shea's first published book. She currently resides in Barrington, New Jersey, where she is working on her second book of poetry.